Cristiano RONALDO

Michael O'Connell

First published in Great Britain in 2006
by Artnik
341b Queenstown Road
London SW8 4LH
UK

© ARTNIK 2006

ISBN 1-903906-76-8

Design: Supriya Sahai
Editor: Will Cain

Printed and bound in Croatia
by H–G Consulting

Photographs courtesy:
Associated Sports Photography

Cristiano
RONALDO

Michael O'Connell

artnik books

The Theatre of Dreams

Somehow, the tough, bruising game of football has evolved into a romance; where a rugged stadium like Old Trafford can, without a hint of embarrassment, be called the Theatre of Dreams. It would make its founders squirm in their graves. Who would have thought that the rowdy fracas that took place on muddy fields in the English countryside, with dozens of people aimlessly chasing an inflated pig's bladder and kicking it as much as each other would one day become the favoured pastime of so many, and the world's 'beautiful game'?

It's unlikely too that anyone who ever played for Newton Heath (L&YR) FC – the works team of the Lancashire and Yorkshire Railway depot at Newton Heath in Manchester – could ever conceive that the club would one day be swallowed up as the personal plaything of an American billionaire and his sons.

Of course, Newton Heath evolved into Manchester United but it wasn't till well over fifty years later that the football that they were playing developed significantly. While Brazilian football, for instance, was becoming something of an art form, English football was about rough-tackling burly men, kicking each other and the ball, which was a heavy, lumpen mass of sodden leather. England was the land of industrial football.

When a Scot named Matt Busby took over the management of Manchester United in 1945, he shocked everyone by becoming involved in training as well as being an administrator. He worked on the ball skills of the players and developed a youth system at the club, which reduced the average age of the first team so dramatically they were called 'the Busby Babes'. His long tenure at the club – punctuated by the Munich Air Disaster – saw United showcase some of the most skilful players of the age. The club also enjoyed unprecedented success.

Busby's greatest discovery was a young man from Northern Ireland called George Best, who became world-renowned for his pace, balance, two-footedness and goal-scoring magic. (Of course, he also became renowned for the partying that killed him at 59.) The managers came and went after Busby but none inherited his mantle until the current manager, Alex Ferguson, bridged the style of United's play over the two eras.

Ferguson has created teams that break quicker than Busby's and which rely upon units of players attacking while exchanging fast, accurate passes. Neither were advocates of that bane of English football, the Route One ball: the endless pumping of long balls into the box where the target man would battle away for the chance of a strike or a lay off. United under both manager liked quick wingers who spread the play wide and got in behind defences. Yet, the one thing that both have liked and which Old Trafford has been weaned on is ball-players who run at defences.

GEORGE BEST
Manchester United

When Busby's scout Bob Bishop discovered George Best, he sent a telegram from Belfast: *I have found a genius*. Best ran at defences and terrorised them.

When Manchester United played Sporting Lisbon in 2003 they came up against a player who did exactly that to them. He, like Geroge Best, had

...pace, balance, two-footedness and goal-scoring magic.

His name was Cristiano Ronaldo and he may just be Manchester United's greatest discovery since the late, great George Best.

The Step-Over Kid

We live in young times, both politicians and football managers strive for the youthful look. Yet, when Cristiano Ronaldo was born (February 5th 1985), Alex Ferguson was about a year away from managing Manchester United: Cristiano's entire life-span covers almost all of his manager's reign at the club. Fergie has a taste for the long haul…he also likes players who show the same long-term commitment to the team as he has the club. United's acquisition of Ronaldo is no flash in the pan.

Cristiano Ronaldo dos Santos Aveiro was growing up in football-mad Portugal. He was born on Madeira, which many on the mainland regard as laughably provincial, but in fact the island is as football-savvy as any of the main cities. Portugal has long been a place where football is revered and a measure of its passionate commitment to the game is its success in staging Euro 2004, beating off neighbouring Spain as well as a few others, despite having only three major cities and ten million inhabitants.

For such a small footballing nation, Portugal has some pedigree, to boot. Three teams have acquired major status: the two from Lisbon, Benfica and Sporting, plus FC Porto. The Portuguese national team have always been renowned for attractive, flowing football, but they have yet to win any tournaments. The most famous Portuguese player ever, of course, is Eusebio – the dynamic forward from the sixties who scored an incredible 727 goals in 715 games for Lisbon's Benfica.

Eusebio

Cristiano grew up with all this football folklore instilled in him by his father Dinis Aveiro and, like him, he came down on the side of Sporting Lisbon when he chose a team. Sporting have lived in the shadow of Benfica, who have been a dominant force since the thirties, but the 'other Lisbon club' have clocked up eighteen league titles in their history, several cups and one European trophy – more than a lot of richer clubs. The fans, like Cristiano and his father, are as dedicated as any in the world.

In a sense, Cristiano's father couldn't help but be football crazy as he actually worked in the game. Dinis was the kit manager for Madeira's local team, Adorinha. Kit managers, even Real Madrid's, are not much more than glorified boot boys and they are paid accordingly. But Dinis had a job and, even if he could only afford to bring up his family in a tin shack, he made it a home that in some ways was as rich as any mansion.

In spite of the poverty, the Aveiros were and are an exceptionally happy family. Cristiano has a brother and two sisters whom he adores; even now, when he is one of the most eligible bachelors in Europe, he says that the only women in his life are his mother and sisters. The story of his success is as uplifting as his talent: he is one of those unique players who when they get the ball create an air of expectancy in the crowd because they might do the impossible.

It was a wonder that his father didn't give him a second name that had something to do with football...

Instead he chose to name him after somebody he was a great fan of – American President Ronald Reagan who was in his second term when Cristiano was born.

Ronaldo is an unusual name in Portugal and, perhaps because of this, the name stuck with Cristiano and even some Manchester United fans today are surprised to learn that Ronaldo is not his surname.

Dinis noticed that his son had a natural flair with a football from an early age. And he wasn't the only one to notice: the family's neighbours saw too that he was special and they later recalled how he spent most of his free time kicking a football around. Over these formative years the skills became silky but no one really expected that he could break out from a backwater like Madeira, which is more famous for its sweet wine than its football.

But Cristiano was obsessed, perhaps more obsessed than his father, and schooling was of little importance to him, much to his family's dismay. For all his father's hopes, both parents were frightened that he would get no further than playing for local teams. They wanted the safety net for him of some qualifications for local the job market. But such was the extravagance of his talent on the football field, inevitably Adorinha grabbed him and gave him an apprentice when he was barely out of short trousers.

Other clubs on the island picked up on Adorinha's acquisition and one offered the equivalent of £270 to his services. Eventually they let him go Nacional – one of the island's biggest clubs – where he got two years of free kit and some professional training.

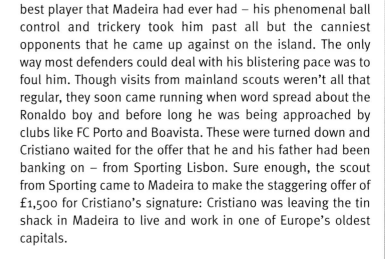

By the time Cristiano was twelve, he was probably already the best player that Madeira had ever had – his phenomenal ball control and trickery took him past all but the canniest opponents that he came up against on the island. The only way most defenders could deal with his blistering pace was to foul him. Though visits from mainland scouts weren't all that regular, they soon came running when word spread about the Ronaldo boy and before long he was being approached by clubs like FC Porto and Boavista. These were turned down and Cristiano waited for the offer that he and his father had been banking on – from Sporting Lisbon. Sure enough, the scout from Sporting came to Madeira to make the staggering offer of £1,500 for Cristiano's signature: Cristiano was leaving the tin shack in Madeira to live and work in one of Europe's oldest capitals.

After interchanging league titles with Benfica for much of the twentieth century, Sporting Lisbon was now really the third in the big three of Portuguese football, with FC Porto having been totally dominant in the nineties when Cristiano joined Sporting. In fact, in recent years it has become famous in football as stopping-off points for the likes of former England manager Sir Bobby Robson, José Mourinho and one of the clubs where United's great keeper Peter Schmeichel played out the end of his career.

This was a unique academy for Cristiano as it would ensure that if his skills delivered on his early promise he would follow in the footsteps of some of Portugal's most fêted footballers.

Sporting has long been celebrated for its football academy, which has produced some of Portugal's greatest footballers, from Eusebio to Luis Figo. For a club of Sporting's comparatively small size, the youth nursery is vital in allowing it to compete above it weight: it nurtured players for its own squad but also ones the club could sell on the transfer market. One club that regularly checked out what the academy had on its books was Manchester United.

It was bound to be a culture shock for this young boy who was just maturing into a gawky teenager. He went from a tiny provincial area to live with some sophisticated youths who couldn't help but make fun of this new entrant's country accent. Already homesick, he was struggling to adapt to the demands of playing as well as keeping up with his other normal studies. These football academies know that only a minority of their pupils will made a living from football and generally they inculcate good academic grades.

It was so bad at one point that even one of his teachers taunted him about his accent and this was one of the first times that the wider world saw the flashes of Cristiano's temper as he threw a chair at the shocked tutor.

Cristiano's individualism on the pitch produced conflicts with his team-mates and, an adolescent growth spurt at 15 that left him looking gawky, made him the butt of country bumpkin jokes. Despite the ridicule, Cristiano stuck to both his unique style of play and ambition of playing for Sporting.

After one season, his growth stabilised and he became more comfortable again and started to impress the coaches. By the time he was 15, he had started to break records for Sporting, becoming the only player in their history to play for the Under-16, Under-17, Under-18, B team and first-team in one season.

He even earned a nickname – 'the new Patrick Kluivert' – because of his strong physical resemblance to the Dutch striker and some of his skills. Even now, though, he had an array of talents that suggested that there would be more to him than Kluivert, a Dutch prodigy who always delivered less than he promised.

Cristiano was now a defender's nightmare with a set of mesmerising tricks to accompany his frightening speed and eye for goal. He certainly was not a kick-and-run merchant whose only trick was the step-over. The point was this dominated his game because more often than not it tricked defenders but he was already demonstrating that when it failed he could twist and turn them as well tempt them into rash tackles. His brakes also matched his acceleration

Of course, Cristiano's forte is still the 'step-over'. It's the kind of trick that nowadays is taught in any coaching academy but it originated in Brazil, as these skills often do, and was made famous by the other Ronaldo, star of the 1998 and 2002 World Cups. In fact, arguably more gifted at this trick was Ronaldo's team-mate, the winger Denilson, last seen by world audiences being chased around the pitch by no less than five Turkish defenders in the closing moments of the 2002 World Cup semi-final. His stand-still step-over, often called the 'Denilson' was his trademark and, for a time, helped make him the most expensive player in the world.

The 'original' Patrick Kluivert

In his early teens, though, Cristiano took the step-over to a higher plain in that he bewitches opponents with a two-footed multiple step-over. Something that is taken for granted in Brazil where players have always been encouraged to use both feet throughout the game, Ronaldo's two-footed ability is still unusual among European professional footballers. The English habit of referring to someone as a 'right-sided' or 'left-sided' player, for instance, is something that mystifies Brazilians.

Cristiano has been able to perfect the stepover using both feet, his boots disappearing into a hypnotising blur as defenders come close – unable to fathom which way he is going to go. It was and is the most special part of Cristiano's repertoire but, unlike Denilson who after a brief flirtation with fame has disappeared from the football radar, he is no one-trick pony. He can suddenly pull out a Cruyff turn or a hook turn; he is also an accurate crosser and passer of the ball. This accuracy translates itself into a readiness to shoot and an ability to score.

His main weakness, which is still there, was he revelled more in the glory of scoring than the accolades of assisting. Glory-hunters get tunnel vision when they get a sight of goal: it is a common fault of individualists and, of course, out-and-out strikers. When he is in a position to shoot, the pure team player will always lay off a ball if someone else is in a better position to score. In a game that is quintessentially a team one, this still remains virtually the council of the gods. Nevertheless, Cristiano's selfish streak has never been such that he plays for himself before he does his team.

Still only in his teens, Cristiano had already carved out a unique roles for himself as a creative midfielder. He frustrated opposition coaches by playing on both wings and providing crosses and passes from his left and right foot: it was a rare thing to see and it made him unplayable.

It was obvious that given Ronaldo's skills he was not going to be in Portugal for very long, it was up to Sporting to get as much out of him as they could before he was transferred. He was barely seventeen when he was thrown into the first team after making his mark in the youth squads but, such was the value put on him by the transfer market, he only ever played 23 times in the Portuguese league.

His league debut came against Moreirense – a perfect start – as he scored two brilliant goals in a 3-0 win. He then went on to score his third goal for the team, a late winner in a 2-1 success over Boavista, something that further endeared him to the Sporting faithful. Moreover, his love for the club was obvious from the start. There was no question that he wouldn't apply himself in every game – so in what seemed like no time at all, he soon heard the notoriously hard-to-please Sporting fans calling for the ball to be passed to him. At the end of the first season playing for Sporting's first team, he had helped them to the top of the league – he had fulfilled a childhood dream when he was still no more than a boy.

Already, the biggest clubs in Europe had been alerted to the boy wonder from Madeira and soon scouts from a number of major clubs were gracing Sporting's stadium in Lisbon. The early favourites to sign Cristiano were Juventus and Liverpool.

When he appeared for Portugal in the U-17 European Championships, the interest in him went to another level. He made a huge impact on the tournament and virtually knocked out the England U-17s on his own. Cristiano was happy with his football but unsettled by the knowledge that while all this interest in him would secure him and his family's future it would also mean him living in another country and learning another language.

Liverpool came very close to making a bid till manager Gerard Houllier had a last-minute change of heart. But as they and others wavered, another English club that had been watching him for months began to close in – Manchester United.

The Other Ronaldo

The year was 2003 and Manchester United had just won the Premiership yet again. Despite this success, all was not really well at the Theatre Of Dreams. The league had been won by sheer persistence as much as skill: they had been chasing a more skilful Arsenal side most of the season and had only managed to pip them at the post when Arsenal fell apart in the last few games.

Their manager, Alex Ferguson, was now in his sixties and many commentators were seeing him and his team as a fading force. After years of rarely-challenged success, Arsenal under the management of Arsène Wenger had emerged as strong rivals to United not only in competition for silverware but also with their attractive, skilful football. Fergie was beginning to look like a manager who was due to spend more time with family.

Commentators pointed to some of his questionable transfer deals. The Argentinian captain, Juan Sebastian Veron, had been bought from Lazio for £28 million, but it quickly became apparent that despite a fairly good start, this artful, refined player was not suited to a sporting life in the hurly-burly of the Premiership.

A Uruguayan striker, Diego Forlan, also arrived. Few had heard of him and, apparently, Ferguson had only ever seen him on video when he sanctioned the purchase. Two and half years and just 10 goals later, Forlan was offloaded to Villarreal, where he scored 25 times in his first season in La Liga!

Ferguson always had a reputation for making astute buys in the transfer market (players who became club legends like Paul Ince, Roy Keane, Andy Cole, Teddy Sheringham and Ruud Van Nistelrooy) and, with his judgement in question, it was time to rediscover his nose for goal-scorers. Especially when he had some vitally important positions to fill.

The 2002/03 season marked the last appearance by David Beckham in ManU colours. The England captain had never played for any other club but the good relationship that he had enjoyed with Alex Ferguson was long gone. Ferguson distrusted the glamourous lifestyle that Beckham had and for a couple of years reports of their training ground bust-ups had been rife. But they reached the point of no return after they lost in the FA Cup to Arsenal that season.

With good cause, Fergie blamed Beckham's slack covering and not tracking back for letting Arsenal score the decisive goal. In the dressing room after the game a boot that Ferguson kicked in fury accidentally hit Beckham in the head and cut his left eyebrow. Beckham's doctor put had two steri-strips – butterfly clips – on the cut and with his Alice band pulling back his hair Beckham chose to parade his injury to the press. Beckham was on his way...

...to Real Madrid, where the marketing potential of the 'galacticos' was eventually to supplant winning silverware. Personally Ferguson did not miss Beckham but professionally he knew United's midfield would. Beckham ran until he dropped and was also the team's dead-ball and set-piece specialist.

Yet, Ferguson was also aware of Beckham's limitations, although a workhorse he had no pace, could not tackle, was not very good in the air and could not beat a man. Fergie was also seeing how other teams were reading Beckham's strengths and countering them. He did not regard Beckham as a spent force but once he decided to sell him he did not look for a replacement similar in style.

Of course, Cristiano Ronaldo's style as a player is quite different from Beckham's but Fergie saw in him a footballer who was a cut above the mould, one who could make things happen. Ronaldo was certainly that – United had been watching him for some time, knowing that at the same time not a few other clubs were too.

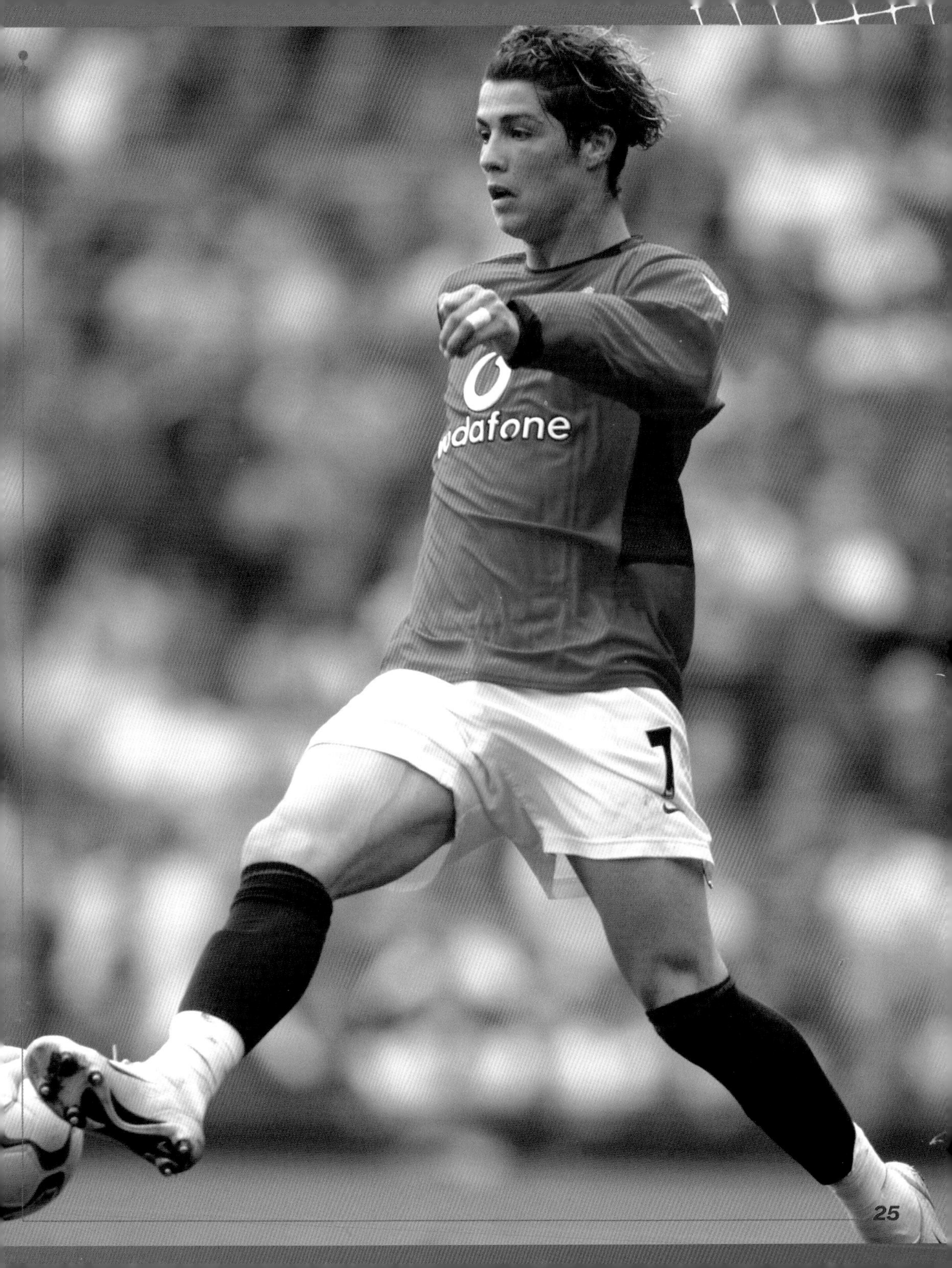
odafone
7

And, as it happened, in that summer of 2003, Manchester United were due to play Sporting Lisbon in a summer friendly, part of the pre-season programme for the impending campaign to retain their title. These friendlies are revenue-spinners, especially as United has a global fanbase and at that stage was the world's richest football club.

The irony was that after United sold Beckham to Real Madrid for £24.5 million the club did not win anything but supplanted ManU as the richest club in the world. Florentino Perez, the president of Real, always boasted that ManU virtually gave Beckham away such was the revenue the club generated from his marketing potential.

United's tour took in the Far East and the United States but Fergie was keen to arrange a game with Sporting to see how Cristiano would shape up to the English style of play. Cristiano knew nothing about it, but the game was effectively arranged as an audition for his possible transfer to Manchester United.

Manchester United are rarely beaten in these kinds of games, as Fergie's competitive nature means he hardly knows the meaning of 'a friendly' and, while he experiments, his team plays to win. On this occasion, however, they lost. Cristiano took the game to them, with Sporting winning 3–1, and Cristiano playing a major part in two of the goals, while completely roasting Gary Neville.

Rather than being sore about being bamboozled by such a young player, the United defenders were all in favour of Sir Alex Ferguson signing him – even though they knew that Sporting might ask a king's ransom for Cristiano's services.

'After we played Sporting the lads in the dressing room talked about Ronaldo constantly,' Ferguson said later. 'And on the plane back from the game they urged me to sign him…'

'That's how highly they rated him.'

It later emerged Fergie had already ensured that United had first refusal on Cristiano, when the wheeling and dealing, which had been going on behind the scenes, was made public. 'We had been negotiating for Cristiano for quite some time,' Ferguson revealed, 'The interest in him from other clubs accelerated in the last few weeks so we had to move quickly to get him.' The sort of money that Sporting were talking about was huge – £12.5 million – but ManU have deep pockets. With the enthusiastic backing of his squad, Ferguson gave the nod to the deal.

For someone who is perceived to rule his teams with a rod of iron, it came as a surprise to some that Ferguson listened so closely to his players on such a talented but unproven entity. Yet it has happened before. The signing of their well-liked Trinidadian forward, Dwight Yorke, in the nineties came about through the United defenders telling Ferguson how much trouble he caused them when he was playing against them at Aston Villa.

Another important factor for Ferguson and United, though, was Cristiano's youth. Ferguson was gradually rejuvenating the ManU squad. The departure of Beckham was something of a watershed as he was one of the earliest links with the days of the midfield that supported Eric Cantona and others up front. Old favourites like Roy Keane and Paul Scholes were either approaching thirty or past it. It was time for a new crop of players to carry the Red Devils' torch. Ferguson placed his faith in Ronaldo becoming one of the leading lights of the club's next generation.

It was a huge responsibility for such a young player, but for the second time in just a few years, Cristiano decided to uproot himself and agreed to sign. He was on his way to the Theatre Of Dreams.

There had been much speculation about who would replace Beckham at Old Trafford. It seemed unthinkable that Ferguson wouldn't go with a big name for the transfer. The early favourite to replace Beckham was Ronaldinho – 'little Ronaldo' – the brilliant young Brazilian forward who many saw as the real star of Brazil's 2002 World Cup victory. Certainly every English fan remembers the way he flummoxed Seaman with a lofted forty-yard free kick that put England out of the quarter finals.

Ronaldinho had let it be known that he was leaving Paris St Germain – where he had played some dazzling football – because of a dispute with the manager over his fondness for partying. Fergie has an aversion to playboy footballers, so it was predictable that he passed on bidding for the Brazilian. While he probably now regrets it, given the way that Ronaldinho has exploded at Barcelona, it is not Fergie's style to admit it. Instead, he was supposed to have turned his attention to one of Cristiano's countrymen, Luis Figo – who was then at Real Madrid.

At that time, Figo was one of the most feared wingers in the game. He had some of Beckham's crossing and free-kick ability, but far more varied wing play, loved taking people on and, although he lacked the real pace, he made up for it by his trickery on the ball. As he and Beckham were both right-sided players, it seemed a plausible scenario for Fergie to part-ex Beckham for Figo.

However, the particular fly in that ointment was that Figo was nearly 30 and, anyway, Fergie was actually eyeing up a young phenomenon called Wayne Rooney who was then playing for Everton. However, to pair Rooney with Ronaldo meant he had to strike a deal first with Sporting and then look to Everton.

Meanwhile, while Fergie liked watching the press following his red herrings, Florentino Perez decided to quell the speculation by announcing his commitment to his 'galacticos' policy. He wanted more stars, not less, and both Figo and Beckham were to be accommodated at Real.

Meanwhile, Ronaldinho went to Barcelona, who were then playing second fiddle to the world's most glamourous club. There was a limit to the number of big names who could replace Beckham to be found in European football and the Manchester United fans really began to wonder – before rumours began to fly among the fans that they had signed Ronaldo from Real Madrid.

Only now people were closing in on the truth as Cristiano was about to be unveiled and news of the 'other Ronaldo' – perhaps Ferguson's most audacious signing – finally came out. Sir Alex Ferguson was well known for promoting youth quickly in his set-up (people like Beckham, the Neville brothers and Paul Scholes all progressed through the United ranks) but he'd never signed such a young player – Cristiano was the world's most expensive teenager in football. It was the most sensational signing of English football in the close season, and in more ways than one.

Ferguson was a product of Scottish football, known as a bit of a bruiser in playing days, but a pretty straightforward player: the relentless attacking of United concealed a cautious, pragmatic side to his football thinking that is often forgotten. It is this combination of adventurous play backed up with the safety net of a fierce midfield work ethic that had brought him huge success. When he reneged on his decision to retire at the end of the 2001/2002 season, it was interpreted as a wish to ensure that when he did hand over the reins of Manchester United their style of play would remain the same.

Ferguson clearly saw Cristiano as a part of that plan. When he inherited the No. 7 shirt, he followed former United luminaries like Eric Cantona, Bryan Robson and George Best. But while Robson and Beckham made their names as midfield workhorses, Ronaldo symbolised a return to creativity and adventure. Best and Cantona would never return to grace the Old Trafford turf but Cristiano ensured that their spirit at least would live on in the Manchester United side.

While the challenge of domesticating Ronaldo's young and unpredictable temperament would be a test of Ferguson's man-management skills, the wise heads remembered how he had tamed people like Ryan Giggs and even Roy Keane in their youth. Manchester United fans, meanwhile, simply looked forward to seeing their newest acquisition's skills at Old Trafford on the first day of the season. After learning he had been handed the iconic shirt at the start of the season, Ronaldo commented: 'The number seven shirt is an honour and a responsibility. I hope it brings me a lot of luck'. And the Gods were certainly smiling on him during his debut.

Aug 16   Manchester United 4-0 Bolton   Premiership 2003/2004

Under Sam Allardyce, Bolton were a steely side adept at snuffing out skillful teams but with players like Jay Jay Okocha and Ivan Campo they also had skill that could win a match against even the most illustrious of opponents. Sam knew about 'the other Ronaldo' but saw nothing in his inclusion on the United bench to cause him to make special provision for the 18-year-old. Cristiano, though, has a habit of making startling debuts and this was to prove no exception.

On 35 minutes, Gigs made his own luck with a free kick that went in off the left upright but to some extent Bolton were still very much in the game until 30 minutes from the end when Fergie subbed Ronaldo for Nicky Butt. Such was the expectation of his appearance that he got a standing ovation from the homeside followers. His first touch of the ball was the signal for another teenager, Alan Hunt, to upend him... however, then it started.

He just caused mayhem in the Bolton defence. The step-overs and the drag-backs were all produced at high speed with defenders backing off almost as fast. He was all over the midfield, too, and very quickly Bolton resorted to the only way to stop him – which was foul him. This earned United a penalty that Ruud van Nistelrooy failed to convert. Nonetheless, he completely unhinged Bolton, and United scored another three before the final whistle. Towards the end the home supporters were chanting, 'There's more than one Ronaldo.'

It was an electrifying debut that made every manager in the Premiership think about how they would stop him doing to their side what he had done to Bolton.

Sept 21 Manchester United 0-0 Arsenal Premiership 2003/2004

It was still sunny in September when Cristiano played one of the biggest games of the season: Manchester United v Arsenal. Billed as 'championship deciders', these matches had developed into handbag showdowns at dawn as each side attempted to tough it out without spilling any blood. Somehow or other the petty disputes had come to overshadow the football...but that also is football

Meanwhile, over at Stamford Bridge changes were occurring that would change the ManU/Arsenal duopoly on the Premiership. In June 2003, Chelsea had been brought by Russian billionaire Roman Abramovich for £60 million, from his fortune which he'd plundered from the state's coffers during the Yeltsin era. The club then went on a £100 million transfer spending spree. Abramovich didn't just want the Premiership, he wanted a super-club and with his money he could afford to settle for nothing less.

Neither side seemed aware that the old order was changing. The players behaved as if the Premiership was owned by them and it should be decided by a playground brawl overseen by Sir [the ref]. For some reason that is not worth explaining, Ruud van Nistelrooy had in Arsenal's eyes become the villain of the piece. Patrick Vieira, Martin Keown and even the normally mild-mannered Freddie Ljungberg had all marked down the Dutch striker as a hate figure, seeing him as over-aggressive towards their team, while diving and play-acting at the slightest hint of aggression directed at him.

On this occasion, Vieira decided that he would show his team-mates how to deal with the Dutchman, which in a phrase was to kick him. If only to confirm his role as villain, when Vieira attempted to kick him but missed, Nistelrooy went down as if he had been hit by a HGV lorry. This of theatre earned Vieira his second yellow.

Even the unflappable Arsène Wenger, called Van Nistelrooy a 'cheat'. As Vieira was the third Arsenal player to be sent off in consecutive fixtures against United, Wenger's outburst begged a few more questions than it purported to answer. Still, while they hadn't been served up much football for their gate money, the fans loved it.

Ironically, Manchester United were awarded a penalty in the closing minutes which van Nistelrooy – their regular penalty-taker – took. For once, nerves got to him, being put off by keeper Lehmann's antics: his shot rattled against the crossbar. At this, the veteran Martin Keown, decided to do his impression of Jack Nicholson in **The Shining**. He leapt off the ground in front of the striker and screamed into his face, goading him about his miss; while the Dutchman, for his part, did a creditable impression of pretending that Keown was not there.

As the whistle blew, it was a signal not for handshakes but more handbag swinging. And where was Cristiano? Rather than standing back and marvelling, he was in the thick of it, as all over the pitch players were clashing. He was later accused (though it was denied) of pushing Martin Keown while he himself was pushed in the back by Ashley Cole, who was among five Arsenal players charged with misconduct. Even Ryan Giggs, who had barely been given a yellow card throughout his career, was involved in an incident, though he escaped charges.

All that aside, Cristiano had performed fairly well on the pitch, though he couldn't make much headway on either wing against full-backs Ashley Cole and Lauren. This was Cristiano's first real taste of the rigours of the Premiership. He knew now that he was looking at a totally different beast from Portuguese football. The games in England were played at a fast and brutal pace – and tackling took no prisoners.

By the 2003/2004 season, the more silky skills of foreign imports had blended with the rough-house play that was still part of our game, making for an intoxicating mix of skill and power. It is this that makes the Premiership the most popular in the world, with crowds roused to passions that Cristiano had not seen in his home country. The slower paced, more technical game of his homeland seemed a world away.

One flaw in his game that was exposed by playing in the Premiership was how Cristiano was following the continental practice of keep-ball rather than moving the ball to forwards quickly and come-what-may. English playmakers push the ball towards forwards within range of scoring even if there is little chance of scoring; whereas Cristiano liked to use his skills to probe for a more telling opening. This gave his play the look of someone who is dribbling for its own sake. The fancy flicks that had impressed everyone to begin with also began to annoy the crowd and he began to be seen as a bit of a show pony. However, his markers kept a much tighter rein on him, which meant the was taking more tumbles – opposition spectators derided him as a diver. Yet even routine Premiership match would leave him with bruises and gashes on his shins.

Of course, he was still adjusting to things other than football. He had left his family behind in Maderia, one of the sunniest places in Europe and found himself in one of the greyest and wettest ones – Manchester United was about the most glamorous thing in Manchester. As he was showing on the football field, he applied himself to adapting to his new way of life. He did, however, say:

'The only thing I can't get used to is the weather and the food.'

Alex Ferguson was keeping a close eye on his prodigy, though, and with a large squad at his disposal, had taken to giving players holidays when he thought they might need it. Cristiano was given three weeks leave and came back rejuvenated for the run-in to the Premiership. But Arsenal were romping away with the title and Chelsea were to push United into 3rd place, which would entail them entering the qualifying stages of the Champions League.

As United's Premiership challenge waned, Cristiano found that he could make his mark in another competition, the one that would make his season – the FA Cup. United were on a good run in a competition, which Sir Alex Ferguson had already claimed five times in his 18 years as manager. Increasingly, it was the big four clubs who had been winning the Cup because most squads, even in the Premiership, just didn't have the resources to sustain a league campaign as well as a cup run. The list of the winners in the last ten years said it all: Everton were the only side outside the big four to have claimed the trophy. Other than on that occasion, it Manchester United or Arsenal or Liverpool or Chelsea.

April 3rd   Arsenal 0-1 Manchester United   FA Cup Semi-Final 2003/2004

United progressed into the semi-finals with ease only to be drawn with their runaway Premiership rivals Arsenal. The match created a lot of interest from the press, mainly for the wrong reasons – namely the anticipation of the game once more degenerating into a kicking match. In fact, it was a chastened Arsenal who were going to be facing United. Five of the players from that kick-about afternoon in September had been disciplined by the FA as well as by the club. Arsenal's directors went on public record to say that matters had got out of hand. Even so the build-up was tense.

Another issue was whether Thierry Henry would be on Arsenal's team sheet. For some years, Arsene Wenger had followed a rotation policy whereby he rested certain players for the FA Cup games: this included swapping goalkeepers so the second-choice player got a rare start, and also preserving their talismanic striker for the more important Premiership games. It was a fairly successful ploy considering Arsenal had already won two FA Cups since Henry had been at the club – but it was obviously a risky strategy in the face of opposition like Manchester United.

It was by far the most eagerly awaited tie of the two semi-finals, and Manchester United were as psyched up as they'd ever been for an FA Cup game. As speculation built up before the game, Alex Ferguson entered the propoganda war by claiming that if Wenger did leave Henry out United would regard it an insult. Whether Wenger even noticed is doubtful.

Arsenal, however, were at full stretch. Their position at the top of the Premiership looked secure – in fact, Arsenal were to go the whole season without defeat – but Wenger was driving them towards the Champions League. Wenger made the decision that the FA Cup was the least important of the three competitions, even though they were going for their third successive FA Cup. He left Henry out of the line-up, putting him on the bench. Whether Fergie regarded that as an insult is also very doubtful.

The game started briskly with Arsenal looking rather edgy without Henry upfront. As one commentator once put, such was Henry's contribution, Arsenal called be called a 'one-player team'. Cristiano made a couple of his trademark runs down the left, renwing his ongoing duel with full-back Lauren. But when they got in a tangle over the ball this time, Lauren helped the Portuguese up from the floor and clapped him round the shoulder in a friendly gesture. There were to be no battles off the ball today.

As for the actual football battles Lauren did not look good against Cristiano, so Ferguson kept him on the same flank for most of the match to exploit the Cameroonian's failings. Soon Cristiano was wreaking havoc – with central defenders Sol Campbell and Kolo Toure forced to cover for Lauren. This skewed their shape at the back. Almost inevitably, the goal originated from Cristiano's side: Gary Neville put aside his simmering feud with Pires to send Ryan Giggs haring into the penalty area, where he crossed to Scholes who hammered the ball past Jens Lehmann. Arsenal rallied with Wenger putting on Henry, Kanu and Reyes in the second half but they had no luck.

Cristiano was on the brink of his first trophy with Manchester United and Fergie had thwarted Wenger again.

May 22nd Manchester United 3–0 Millwall
Cup Final 2004

Standing in his and Manchester United's way was a side that were the antithesis of the new, flambuoyant and attacking style that Ferguson instilled with the purchase of Cristiano. Millwall were the surprise of the 2004 FA Cup, bulldozing their way into the Final with a string of performances that belied their Championship status. Spearheaded by the veteran Dennis Wise, formerly of Chelsea, they represented old-style industrial English football and nobody gave them any chance against United and that is how it turned out. It was a one-sided match with Millwall looking to no more than clogging up the midfield and hope some loast cause would find a home in United's goal. Dennis the Menace chopped and hacked any United player who got near him – even Keane gave him a wide berth – but it was always a question of not whether United would win but by how many.

From the whistle United poured forward, especially down the flanks, and Cristiano was was running riot. Cristiano's flashy array of skills wreaked havoc in Millwall defence but spectators in the Millennium Stadium could see that for all his flamboyance and razzle-dazzle Cristiano was the real deal. Ferguson and his coaching staff had turned the show pony into a thoroughbred.

For all Cristiano's creative endeavours, the first goal was scored rather than provided by him. From a Keane through ball, Gary Neville overlapped down the right flank and, as he shaped up to cross, Cristiano trotted into the penalty area behind Dennis Wise, who was ball-watching. As the ball came over an unmarked Cristiano had a free header: he netted for the first goal on the stroke of half time.

Now that the Millwall defences had been breached, the floodgates opened and United rained down shots on Andy Marshall's goal. The Millwall keeper saved his side from an embarrassing scoreline. With two goals from van Nistelrooy, one a penalty and the second, on 81 minutes, a poacher's goal on the right side of the 6-yard box from a Giggs' cross. All that remained was for the Millwall's player-manager-captain, whose tackling had increasingly turned to getting the man rather than the ball, to be subbed before he exhausted the ref's forebearance and was red-carded. Wise left the pitch like the head boy being sent to the dunce's corner.

While some United supporters had, at the start of the season, questioned Alex Ferguson's judgement in replacing Beckham with Cristiano, his performance in the Cup Final answered the critics in spades.

As one match commentator put it, Ronaldo...

'...proved his credentials to wear the famed Manchester United number seven shirt with a dazzling FA Cup-winning display against an outplayed Millwall side.'

Though United had lost out on the title to an Arsenal side who overpowered teams with their slick teamwork and passing, this United team-in-transition were still capable of claiming an important trophy (bagging the Arsenal scalp along the way, of course). Cristiano Ronaldo was symbolic of this transitional stage and he had played a major role in bringing another trophy to Old Trafford.

The manager and the team were quick to pay tribute to Cristiano saying that he was the future of Manchester United. Still only nineteen, Cristiano was ecstatic in his celebrations for more than one reason: with this performance, he had almost certainly booked his place in the Portugal team for the Euro 2004 championship – in Portugal.

esplendor de Portugal

tre as brumas da memória

Pátria sente-se a voz

os teus egrégios avós

ue há-de guiar-te

s armas! As armas

obre a terra, sobre

As armas! As arma

Pela Pátria lutar

Contra os canhões

Desfralda a invicta b

À luz viva do teu céu

Brade a Europa à terra intei

Portugal não pereceu!

Beija o solo teu jucundo

O oceano a rujir d'amor,

teu braço vencedor

Euro 2004

An elite footballer can play his whole career without appearing in a major international competition on home soil. Cristiano Ronaldo did it after his first full season in senior football. Not only was he in the Portugal squad, he had more than a chance of a medal as his team were one of the favourites to win the 2004 European Championships.

Arséne

Wunderkinds are nothing new in football, of course. Pelé lit up Brazil's victory in the 1958 World cup when he was only 17. However, Euro 2004 had two: no only Cristinao but also Wayne Rooney for England. They were both touted by their countries' respective fans as potential matchwinners.

Wayne Rooney was 8 months younger than Cristiano but apart from their age and their talent on the football pitch they had nothing else in common. They look as different as they play: Rooney a dray and barnstorming second striker; Ronaldo a thoroughbred and dribbling winger. Whereas Ronaldo stepped out with catwalk models, Rooney seemed more at home in the massage parlours of Liverpool's Toxteth. Yet, unknown to both, as they played for their different countries, Alex Ferguson was already scheming to bring both under his wing at Manchester United.

Rooney was currently at Everton but the club had neither the money nor chance of European football to keep their only jewel in the crown. It would take Fergie more than two months of wheeling and dealing to secure Rooney for United. But such was his conviction that with Rooney complementing Ronaldo he would be able upstage the new Premiership duopoly of Arsenal and Chelsea, not even Abramovich and Wenger combined would have been able to thwart the wiley Scot.

Portugal had been a surprise choice by FIFA to host the European Championships, beating off some stiff competition but as it was one of the poorest countries in the EU the prospect of this football bonaza was welcomed by the population. Football hooliganism is small beer compared with the tourist boom and stimulus to the overall economy that such a tournament creates.

The Portugal team were also better placed to win the competition than ever before. In Euro 2000, co-hosted by Belgium and the Netherlands, they had impressed everyone with their skill and drive: Nuno Gomes, at the age of 23, had been the revelation in that tournament. They also boasted the likes of Luis Figo, Rui Costa and a host of other creative players who helped Portugal electrify the tournament. They went out in the semi-finals to eventual winners France but along the way they beat England 3–2.

But this Euro 2004 team was even better. Figo was still there and without the pace of old but any player who could regularly make Real Madrid's team sheet was still something special. Nuno Gomes remained in the line-up, along with Pauleta, Deco, Maniche and a host of other players plucked from elite clubs in Portugal and the rest of Europe – including, of course, Cristiano Ronaldo.

To make the home nation's chances even better, marshalling all these players was Luis Felipe Scolari, the World Cup winning manager of Brazil in 2002. When he took over as Brazil coach, 'Big Phil' had infuriated the country's fanatical supporters by curbing the inidvidualism and flair that had long been the hallmark of Brazilian football. His admission that he admired the organisation and industriousness of English football was almost sacrilege. Yet, he knew that international competitions were no longer won by teams with highly-skilled members all playing to their own strengths. He installed a more pragmatic, defensive attitude in his players, many of whom since they were playing for top European clubs took readily to his methods. However, it took Brazil's victory in the 2002 World Cup for the Brazilian public to warm to his approach.

Scolari had been snapped up by the Portugese in 2003 especially for European Championship and coming into the tournament his record had not exactly been spectacular: seven victories, five draws and two defeats. But he had managed to pull off a home 2–1 win over Brazil!

He saw in Ronaldo exactly the problem that he had confronted in his early days with Brazil. Freed from the discipline of Fergie's United, Ronaldo had reverted in training to his more expressive, free-wheeling style of play Consequently, Scolari put Ronaldo on the bench for the opening game against Greece – a raucous curtain raiser for the tournament in that the home side were expected to roll over the Greeks. Greece were a side with no international pedigree, made up a team of journeyman players in a group that also featured fellow favourites and Portugal's great rivals, Spain.

June 12th   Portugal 1-2 Greece   Euro 2004 Opening Match

Scolari ran into the kind of brick wall that he had never run into when he was managing Brazil. The Greeks, as their qualifying matches had already shown, were now very physical, well-drilled and weren't going to give Portugal any space to play open, free-flowing football. Their coach Otto Rehhagell had introduced man-marking and a sweeper to clamp down on the ball-players. Ironically, Rehhagel was singing from the same hymn sheet as the newly celebrated Portuguese uber-coach José Mourinho, whose use of similar tactics had won the Champions League for lowly FC Porto.

When the whistle blew for the game to start, the home fans were already baying for the expected goal from the home side. However, the Greeks had not read the script: they nearly scored in the opening minute when Angelos Charisteas on the edge of the 8-yeard box just failed to get on the end of cross. Then, five minutes later, they did score when Giorgos Karagounis pounced on a mistake by Paulo Ferreira and drove a 25-yard shot past goalkeeper Ricardo. The crowd were stunned and the opening-match nerves of the home team only intensified. The rest of the first half saw the Greeks frustrate everything that Portugal attempted... Scolari knew that he had to take a risk. He decided to put on two flair players, Deco, the creator supreme for FC Porto in the Champions League – and Cristiano.

Cristiano stepped out with Deco as the country's saviours and the crowd willed their team on once more: 1–0 down at half-time requires only one answer – a quick goal after the restart. But the Greeks were determined to spoil the party and 6 minutes after the re-start, they were on the attack again and in dangerous territory. They forced themselves into the box and one of the Portuguese tracking back made a desperate, rather foolish challenge. It was Cristiano.

The iconic Italian referee Pierluigi Collina pointed automatically to the penalty spot and Cristiano held his head in his hands. This was not the way that his triumphant homecoming was supposed to unfold.

The utterly unthinkable was now confronting Portugal as Angelos Basinas confidently tucked penalty into the top right-hand corner of the net. The Portuguese were frenetic in their attempts to retrieve the game but as the clock ticked down the Greek's brick wall stood firm. Cristiano, desperate for some kind of redemption, Deco and a sorely peeved Figo all tried to fashion chances. As added time was played out, when the chance of even a draw was already long gone, Cristiano managed to get his head on a cross from Figo to score a consolation goal for Portugal. Not that it consoled the country's 50,000 fans in the spectacular Dragao Stadium, home to FC Porto.

Portugal v Russia

It was almost a national disaster for Portugal and a personal nightmare for Cristiano. He had come to Euro 2004 with the nation's hopes on his shoulders, then before his own people in his first international in the European Championship, he had given away the penalty that effectively sealed their defeat.

Scolari said, 'I'm beaten down, sad, but these results happen.' He added, 'The next game is life or death for us.'

June 17 Portugal 2–0 Russia Euro 2004

The next game was against what was possibly an even more pragmatic team but Scolari decided his side had to play with a more offensive spirit than they had against Greece. Cristiano was left on the bench again and didn't see any play until the 78th minute. The Portuguese were still nervy and, despite the Russian goalkeeper, Sergei Ovchinnikov, being sent off for handling outside his area, they had to largely rely on the inspiration of Figo, having one of his best games ever in a Portuguese shirt, to win the game. Maniche settled some of the nerves with a well-taken goal in the seventh minute, but the fans had to wait a long time for the game to be put beyond doubt. They did it soon after Cristiano made his entrance. A superb cross found fellow substitute Rui Costa who converted from close range.

Portugal had their campaign back on track, but they were about to face the toughest team in the group – their great rivals, Spain. And they had to win.

June 20th Portugal 1-0 Spain Euro 2004

Spain needed a draw to go through to the quarter finals; Portugal had to win. However, Portugal had not beaten Spain since 1981, and Spain's manager, Inaki Saez, now had one of the strongest squads in years. Most of his best players were from Barcelona and Real Madrid: Carlos Puyol, the powerhouse full back, the brilliant goalkeeper Iker Casillas and the inspirational striker's striker Raul. The match promised to be an unnerving encounter but hanging over Scolari was the 3–0 hammering that Spain had inflicted on Portugal the previous September.

He decided to gamble on including Cristiano from the start. It was a fair bet to make as the imperatives of progessing to the quarter-finals meant that Spain were likely to be defensive whereas Portugal had to attack. Scolari knew the tentative performances that Portugal had produced so far were unlikely to unsettle Spain. With Figo leading the way on the right, it made sense to unleash the dazzling ballplay of Ronaldo on the left, although putting an untried 19-year-old into Portugal's biggest ever game was not without its risks.

The omens were good for Ronaldo. The match was being played at the new Estádio José Alvalade, the home ground of Sporting Lisbon, its inaugaural match the previous August was the friendly between Sporting and Manchester United. This was the game in which Ronaldo turned Gary Neville inside out and precipitated Fergie's bid.

Although the match was touted as one of the tournament's possible goal-fests, against that was the implications of the requirements to qualify for the knock-out stage. And so it proved to be: each side preferring to get men back rather than forward. After 15 minutes each team had created just one chance each. But Cristiano and Figo were working the flanks remorelessly and Deco was pulling most of the strings in the centre of the park.

Portugal v Spain

Cristiano created an early chance for Figo with a mesmerising run at Spain's defence but Figo's shot was blocked by Ivan Helguera. Spain flunked a similar chance. Then, on the stroke of half time, a glancing header of Cristiano's from a Figo cross went just wide of the upright.

Scolari withdrew Pauleta Resendes at the interval and replaced him with another striker, Nuno Gomes. The substitution turned the tables: 12 minutes into the half the Benfica striker took a pass from Figo on the edge of the 18-yard area, turned and shimmied for some space, then rifled a low shot into the corner of the net.

Spain threw everything into attack with Saez making three substitutions, but Portugal kept their shape and advantage. Waiting for them in the quarter-finals was England and Wayne Rooney.

England, like Portugal, had perhaps their best chance for many years of winning a major tournament. Under the management of Sven-Goran Eriksson, they were a revitalised outfit: they had been forced out of the World Cup in 2002 largely because of the incomparable skill of Brazil's Ronaldinho but for this tournament they had added immeasurably to their firepower with Eriksson's early introduction of the 18-year-old Rooney into international football. Rooney was a forceful support striker who perfectly complemented the consummate poaching skills of Michael Owen. Where Owen might seem out of the game for long stretches and prowled the furthest reaches of the pitch, Rooney was a bundle of energy who loved to pick up the ball from deep areas and take on players. He had brought more or less instant results.

Where Cristiano started on the bench for Portugal, it was virtually unthinkable for Eriksson to name Rooney as a sub. The impact he had made domestically and internationally was spectacular. His first game in Euro 2004 was against favourites France, when he was wonderfully composed against a side boasting the likes of Zinedine Zidane, Thierry Henry and David Trezeguet. England were the underdogs in the game but they went ahead through a Frank Lampard header. It might have been more when Rooney won a penalty, but that was brilliantly saved. It all went horribly wrong in the closing minutes, however, when England gave away first a free kick and then a penalty for which Zidane mercilessly punished them.

They were now in more or less the same position as Portugal had been after their opening match, though they had less formidable opponents in Switzerland and Croatia. Both games were a triumph for Rooney: he scored in the first, becoming the youngest ever player to score in a European Championship, and then scored twice in the demolition of Croatia, walking off with the Man of the Match award. Going into the quarter final with Portugal, he was the talk of the tournament, but many commentators were keen to draw comparisons with these two wunderkinds of the game, with Rooney, at the moment, overshadowing Cristiano.

The England v Portugal game was undoubtedly the high spot of the tournament. The control, poise and flair of the Portuguese were the perfect counterpoint to the powerful, fast-moving and direct play of England, who under Sven-Goran Eriksson were now showing a sureness on the ball. Scolari went with Cristiano again, but in order to pit Cristiano against Arsenal's Ashley Cole he switched their flanks. He knew how Cristiano had tormented Cole in the Premiership. He also ordered his defence to mark Rooney, who had already scored four goals, out of the game.

As the game started, the Portuguese defence were constantly being pulled out of shape by the focus on Rooney: so much so that Michael Owen was being allowed far too much space. After just three minutes he latched on to a mistake by Costinha and finished clinically. Costinha who was trying to head the ball back to his goalkeeper, however as the ball dropped over Portugal's defenders Owen pounced, turned and chipped the ball over the keeper Ricardo. It was a poacher's goal but for all that one that was pure class.

England were in the driving seat already and Rooney had hardly had a touch. Rooney, however, was then involved in a challenge for a loose ball with Jorge Andrade and fractured a matatarsal bone in his foot – he came off after 27 minutes to be replaced by Darius Vassel. Portugal pressed England but despite some wayward passing from Frank Lampard and Paul Scholes held onto their lead.

It was noticeable that for all Cristiano's efforts to repeat his roasting of Cole the Arsenal left back was not for turning twice. Cristiano tried every trick he could but it was like seeing a snake-charmer failing to mesmerise: Cole kept his eye locked on the ball every time and simply cut out Cristiano from the game. After the match even Cristiano's ManU team-mate Gary Neville was unstinting in his praise for Cole.

In the second half, Portugal kept up their unrelenting pressure and, then, Scolari subbed Costinha and Figo who showed his fury at his undignified exit by his demeanour and exit, going straight down the tunnel to the changing rooms and not to the Portugal dugout.

In their place, Scolari bought on Simao Sabrosa and Helder Postiga.

Beckham misses the penalty

The minutes ticked by in the second half as England hung on grimly. But the equaliser paid tribute to Scolari's uncanny nose for substitutions: within 8 minutes Simao put a corner in, which was cleared back to him, from his second cross Postiga headed an unstoppable past David James. Just before the end Sol Campbell thought like he'd wrapped up the match when he bundled in a rebound off the bar, but Terry was adjudged to have fouled the keeper. It was extra time.

In the second period of extra time, Rui Costa gathered the ball on the edge of the penalty box and blasted it in off the crossbar into James' net. However, England equalised 5 minutes later in a goalmout melee, after a Beckam corner, when from inside the 6-yard box Frank Lampard banged home John Terry's knock-down.

Penalty shoot-out.

The stadium was a cauldron of nerves, which Eusabio stirring in the crowd only intensified. Beckham took the first and

bottled it over the bar. However, Rui Costa rescued him from the doghouse by missing Portugal's third. Cristiano's was one of the most confidently-taken of the lot. He wheeled away in celebration when he scored: he'd proved that he had all the composure of the man he had replaced at Manchester United and some more.

It went to six and Darius Vassell drove a low ball to the keeper's left but Ricardo Pereira read him and saved. Ricardo then took the next penalty and coolly dispatched it for a Portugal win. They deserved to. The stats said it all: possession 61%, shots 35 to England's 16, fouls 14 to 25.

Portugal were into the semi-final.

The celebrations were enough to make people believe the competition itself had been won but Cristiano summed up the huge effort that the team had made:

'We showed great grit, determination and confidence and over the 120 minutes we showed we had the confidence to win the game.'

Scolari noted: 'All wins are delicious, but this one – especially after everything that happened – was spectacular.'

June 30th Portugal 2–1 Holland
Euro 2004 Semi-Final

The pedigree couldn't get much better: Holland. The Dutch team had looked below par on their way to yet another semi-final in a major tournament, but they still had the quality to make it this far with people like Ruud Van Nistelrooy, Edgar Davids and Patrick Kluivert. Portugal were perceived to have made hard work of getting this far and they were the definite underdogs in a match that would mark Cristiano's highspot in the competition.

From the moment the game started it was clear that the Portuguese were better motivated, which was not surprising given the fanatical home support, while the Dutch were out of sorts. There were rumours of internal unrest within the squad, something that was becoming an occupational hazard for Holland in international tournaments. Where Cristiano had undoubtedly met his match in the last game, he was now bouncing back against the Dutch, alive with ideas – as was Luis Figo. Disappointed at being substituted against England, Figo had a point to prove and almost overshadowed the compelling trickery of Cristiano with an epic 70-yard run that scythed through Dutch defence and very nearly produced a goal.

Then came Cristiano's moment of glory. In the 26th minute in what was almost a carbon copy of his goal against Millwall in the FA Cup Final, he took up an unassuming position for a corner, only to make a beeline for the goal. Figo arced the ball perfectly into his path and Cristiano's powerful header beat goalkeeper Edwin van der Sar. All of a sudden, he was whipping off his shirt and sending hearts fluttering as he celebrated wildly. For the first time in the tournament, the Portuguese looked like they were fulfilling their rich potential – and Cristiano hadn't finished yet.

Portugal won a corner in the 58th minute which Ronaldo jogged over to take. As the Dutch waited for a delivery into the box, he produced an ingenious short pass which gave Maniche time to take aim. Despite a tight angle, he produced a powerful curling shot that beat the keeper and left the Dutch defence looking accusingly at each other.

The Dutch got one back, an own goal from Jorge Andrade just after the hour, but this was Portugal's and Cristiano's night. The game finished 2–1, with some of the Dutch admitting they had deserved to lose. Cristiano was named Man of the Match.

The fairy tale did seem to be coming true after all. While Wayne Rooney was nursing an injury and watching Euro 2004 on TV, the step-over kid from Madeira was now one of Portugal's most celebrated footballers on the brink of a major final.

Only Eusebio and Luis Figo were more famous than this nineteen-year-old who was quickly transformed into a national treasure. His place in the Euro 2004 final was now assured, with Scolari's faith again repaid. Figo, too, was being lionised as he prepared to win his final cap for Portugal. Destiny seemed to dictate that this was Portugal's year.

Incredibly, it was the Greeks, they would face in the final – their opponents in the opening match, who had somehow made it all the way to the final. The Greeks had followed their victory over the Portuguese with their by-now familiar gritty displays against Russia and Spain. It had been enough of a shock that they had beaten Portugal, and even more of a surprise that they had come through the group stages at Spain's expense. But no one gave their industrial football a chance against the French in the quarter finals.

Even so, the august assembly of Zidane, Henry and a dazzling assembly of stars from the major European teams could find no way past Rehhagel's well-drilled, disciplined crew. Angelos Charisteas scored the only goal in a 1–0 win. With no recognised world class player, everyone drawn largely from the two big Athens teams or unheralded clubs around Europe, Rehhagel has produced a coaching miracle and laid down a benchmark in how to make the beautiful game ugly.

They beat a free-scoring Czech side 1–0 on the silver goal rule in the semi-finals. They did to them what they did to everyone they met: they pressurised all the time, closed players down and forced errors, but when a chance was on, they seemed to come alive. And someone always scored. They had done it to the Portuguese, the Spanish, the French and now the Czechs – and still no one gave them a chance in the final.

Groundhog Day in international football came with a flurry of patriotic fervour in Portugal, the eyes of the nation on their wunderkind Cristiano, led by his wundervater, Luis Figo. It was the first time in any international championship that the two team that opened the tournament met in the final. This time nearly 65,000 spectators watched the game from Benfica's fabulous Estádio da Luz (Stadium of Light).

As the game opened, with both the Portugal team and the watching nation knowing they faced an endurance test that might not end until the penalty shoot-out. From the outset, the Greeks played the way Otto Rehhagel had drilled them: man-marking in the last third of the pitch, tracking back immediately they lost the ball, keeping their own attacks to Route One ventures. Scolari threw everything he had at them but everything was absorbed by the Rehhagel tactics with only the occasional threat to the Greek goal. When there was a threat keeper Nikopolidis was more than up to the task of keeping a clean sheet. It didn't matter that the Greeks stifled the football out of the game because the drama and tension was spectacle enough. It struck one English commentator that this was Roundheads against Cavaliers and we know who won that war.

A goal-less first half...then in the second on the 57th minute Greece won their first corner. One could almost hear the clanging bell of doom before the Greek cheers when Charisteas scored from it – Greece's one and only on-target attempt on goal. Scolari urged the Portuguese on. Cristiano came as close as anyone, first with a twenty-yard drive that was saved and, then, having been put through one-on-one with the keeper, he managed to shoot over the bar to moans of stoic despair. Figo made himself a perfect opening in the closing stages, only to see his shot pass a few inches wide of the post.

It was going to be a Roundhead day.

As the final whistle blew, Otto Rehhagel broke down in tears as did Cristiano Ronaldo...

The Boy Grows Up

Sadly, for the next eighteen months or so, it was less and less of a fairytale for Cristiano, although there was the compensation of the odd fantastic moment. With the rest of Portugal, he watched enviously as the celebrations in Greece went on for a few days but at least he had the consolation that he had announced himself on the world stage and was now a regular in the Portugal side. In the coming months, Portugal gradually regrouped under Scolari and began to make their way towards the World Cup in Germany in 2006.

Things were also breaking well on the home front. Fergie pulled out his trump card for the 2004/05 Premiership – Wayne Rooney. Just as Sporting had had to sell Cristiano so with Everton and Rooney: it was always a question of when and how much. Not that the supporters or management appreciated that, and efforts were to keep him at Everton. However, after a bit of a Dutch auction with Newcastle, at the end of August Fergie got Rooney for roughly £27 million, a few hours before the close of transfer deadline. Since some of the clauses of the deal relate to performance the eventual cost will probably be a bit more than that, but whatever the final figure it will be more than double what Cristiano cost.

Rooney came to the club still nursing a broken metatarsal bone and did not make his début for the club until 28 September 2004 in the UEFA Champions League against Fenerbahçe; he scored a hat-trick and also an assist (the match finished in a 6–2 win for United). His performance was as spectacular as the stats suggest. He was clearly going to be a massive asset for United, and at £27 million a bargain to boot. Ronaldo stayed on the bench for this match but Old Trafford was agog with how well they would combine together. They only had to wait a week, when United played host to Middlesbrough.

In fact, Rooney was smothered by a well-drilled Boro defence, whereas Ronaldo bamboozled the cover. Fergie anxiously prowled the manager's box on the touchline as his investments in the future went through their paces. It was from one of Ronaldo's bullet crosses that sub Alan Smith headed United's equaliser. Whatever the day's result or the performance of the pair it was evident that Arsenal and Chelsea had company.

Chelsea were still spending but not as much as in the Claudio Ranieri era. He had gone – Abramovich had decided that £100 million spent on the transfer market should secure more than runner-up in the Premiership and a semi-final place in the Champions League. After toying with Eriksson, Abramovich replaced Ranieri with José Mourinho who had just taken lowly FC Porto to winning the Champions League... beating Monaco at, coincidentally, Stamford Bridge. It didn't take Mourinho long to dip into Abramovich's war chest: he spent £24 million on Marseille's Didier Drogba and £20 million on Porto defender Ricardo Carvalho. Waching all this an appalled Arsène Wenger called it 'financial doping'.

Brimming with confidence and tactical awareness, Mourinho had studied the Premiership and had already decided that Alex Ferguson rather than Arsène Wenger was the manager to respect. But both their teams had to be beaten to win the Premiership. Mourinho's first encounter with United and, he assumed, Ronaldo was on August 15 before Fergie secured Rooney.

Aug 15th Chelsea 1–0 Manchester United Premiership 2004/05

United were plagued with injuries and were without Rooney and Ronaldo, absences in the backline also pushed Keane into a defensive role. Chelsea secured an early lead with Eidur Gudjohnsen bundling the ball in and, after that, Mourinho's new team never once looked likely to allow their advantage to slip. They always had at least 5 players behind the ball and when they lost possession were fast and disciplined in pulling back and closing down space. Chelsea now played slightly differently to whatever club they were against and also changed their shape according to whether they were drawing, in front or behind. It wasn't Greek-style or industrial football – Mourinho had too much talent in his squad for that – but it was controlled, methodical and tactical.

The most animated aspect of Chelsea's game was Mourinho's act on the touchline: his emotions very much on the sleeves of his overcoat, lolling smugly on the bench one moment, jumping up and throwing up his arms in despair at the next. One thing was obvious he was going to deliver the Premiership on a plate to the watching Roman Abramovich who sat in the director's box with a look of childlike entrancement on his face. He was like a little boy in the toyroom whose tin soldiers had suddenly come to life.

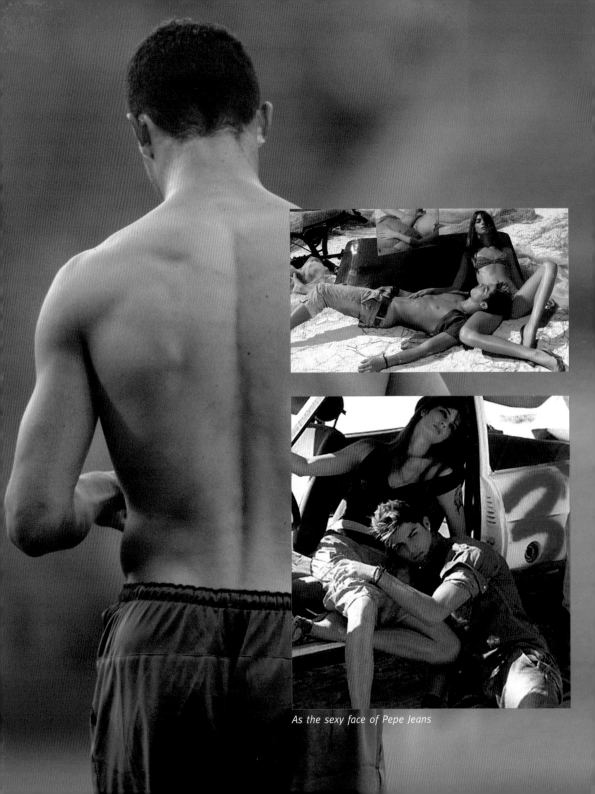

As the sexy face of Pepe Jeans

Oct 24th Manchester United 2-0 Arsenal Premiership 2004/05

Arsenal came to Old Trafford top of the Premiership, 11 points clear of United and looking like they would extend their record-breaking unbeaten run to 50. Fergie had other ideas. He doesn't like France, French food, French people and most of all a particular French manager. He once invited Arsène Wenger to a post-match drink and the Frenchman declined. For Fergie one highlight of any season is beating Arsenal.

Ronaldo was on fire and the only way Arsenal could deal with him was by chopping him down. Ashley Cole went in late almost immediately, before the Neville brothers also had a turn each. The Iberian peninsular seemed to bring up the red mist on both sides as United directed their attentions to Jose Reyes. Both Fergie and Wenger remonstrating furiously from their respective boxes on the touchline over the incompetence of referee Mike Riley.

Riley did book both Neville's for taking a bite out of Ronaldo's legs but the game continued without anyone being carried off on stretcher or, in fact, red-carded until Vieira got his marching orders late in the match. Despite looking the more likely to score, Arsenal didn't and it wasn't until 73 minutes that United opened accounts. Wayne Rooney hurdled Sol Campbell's challenge but suckered Riley into awarding a penalty. Well, that not how Wenger put it, given that this was Riley's 5th penalty for United in his last 6 visits to Old Trafford.

Nistelrooy tucked it away, with Lehmann going the wrong way. By now Ronaldo was reduced to being a passenger and was subbed by Alan Smith. Reyes had also been taken off some 10 minutes earlier. In stoppage time, Smith set up Rooney for his first Premiership goal for United. It was his 19th birthday.

On the cover of the Portuguese edition of GQ magazine

Campbell and Rooney were still slagging each other off as they went down the tunnel to the changing rooms. Wenger was going on about how van Nistelrooy 'cheats' and moaning about United's physical game. Ferguson stated shouting at him to shut up and take Arsenal's loss like a man: unusually for Wenger he virtually squared up to him. Some of the Arsenal players, who were already in their changing room, picked up some of the interval refreshments and threw them at Fergie. The 'Battle of the Buffet' as it became known had been joined.

Fergie ended up with pea soup on his suit and shirt. As is his habit on occasions when Arsenal are under investigation, Wenger reached for his white stick: 'I don't know about food throwing. I did not see if something was thrown.' By all accounts, it was instigated by 17-year-old Cesc Fabegras, who'd stayed on the bench. Thankfully, no one had a handbag to throw... not even Ashley Cole.

Cristiano had been in the thick of the battle on the pitch, taking more flak than he gave. Fergie said of his game, 'Of course, Cristiano still has a lot to work on. It is easy to forget that he is only 19. He is still very strong mentally and he is tough – there is no doubt about that.' However, a week later he was back in the team for United's 2–0 defeat at the hands of Pompey, but this was around the time that Chelsea began to assert their hold over the Premiership and ManU dropped off the pace. What was equally evident was the Ronaldo and Rooney were going to be a double-thorn in the side of any defence. In March of the following year, Fergie said:

'We are very fortunate to have these two young players. They are both in fantastic form at the moment and along with Ronaldinho, I think they will become the best players in the world in a couple of years' time.'

Although Cristiano came to United on a fairly modest salary of £25,000 per week he was clearly destined to be become very wealthy. Even when the trickery does not deliver end product, his flamboyant style catches the eye; he is also very good looking, which his goal celebrations of whirling his stripped-off shirt only emphasise. His agent Jorge Mendes, who also represents José Mourinho, was soon building up a formidable ancillary rights portfolio: he now endorses Nike, Pepe Jeans and Suzuki cars. All of this also made him a sex symbol in Portugal... for both sexes. **PortugalGay** voted him the sexiest player on the Portuguese national team. Yet, he is not all playboy footballer.

Three weeks after the tsunami disaster of Boxing Day 2004, an 11-year-old Indonesian boy named Martunis was spotted by a British television helicopter crew on a Banda Aceh beach.

He had survived by eating dried noodles and drinking rainwater. When they went down to rescue him they found that he was wearing the Portuguese national team football jersey, which touched Cristiano to the core. 'This really got to me, after seeing the images I was really touched,' he said. It got to everyone else in the squad, including Scolari, and their intervention resulted in a massive influx of aid.

Martunis with his father and (left) with Luis Figo.

He became involved in raising money for the survivors and personally adopted the cause of Martunis. He struck up a strong relationship both the boy and his father, who also survived, and by June he had covered all their expenses and had the football-mad pair flown out to attend one of Portugal's World Cup qualifiers. Subsequently all the players in the squad, thanks to Cristiano's encouragement, contributed money to buy them a house in Indonesia – Cristiano also raised money for the charity he was working with by auctioning off all his personal sports clothes.

United were clearly not going to catch Chelsea in the Premiership nor, as it turned out Arsenal either, which left the club chasing the Champions League and the FA Cup. However, they went to Highbury on February 1 and achieved the double for the season with a 4–2 victory thriller that was rough and tough but a cornucopia of skill. The match actually began in the tunnel with Vieira and Keane shaping up to each other: incredibly, with 6 yellows, one red and numerous flashpoints, both captains left the field without being booked.

Ronaldo was but for an over-exuberant celebration of his second goal by way of roostering before the Arsenal fans. He played a blinder, which Fergie celebrated a couple of days later. He said, 'When we bought Ronaldo we bought him purely for his ability. The Sporting Lisbon youth coach said to us way back that everything was right about him. But we didn't realise what a great warrior he was... It wasn't an easy game but it was a fantastic performance and I was proud of the way my young players like Ronaldo handled it.'

The three points gave United a sniff of catching Chelsea but, in fact, they ended the season in third place. They were also snuffed out of the Champions League in the last sixteen by AC Milan who saw them off with 1–0 victories both at Old Trafford and the San Siro. It didn't help that the two goals were scored by Mourinho-reject Hernan Crespo. Although the 16.8 million Argentine striker – signed by Ranieri and loaned to AC Milan – came back to Chelsea the next season and performed well enough for Mourinho to decide to keep him.

Ronaldo was finding his feet in the Premiership. There had been dips in form and controversy over his tendency to dive at the touch of defender but Fergie was bringing him along. In June, Giggs was to speak insightfully of Fergie's coaching:

'I can see similarities in how the manager handled me to the way he is handling Cristiano. Every time he has a good game he wants to play again – fans want him to play and deep down the manager probably wants him to, as well. But you have to look at the bigger picture. To get the best out of Cristiano,he needs rest at the right points.

'It's not just physical, it's mental as well. There were times the manager did it with me. Cristiano has probably found it hard to understand at times. **But it is purely to do with his development and, over the next three or four years, I'm certain he will become a great player.'**

Fergie was concerned about the fact that at this period Ronaldo was the most fouled player in the Premiership. He spoke about the cup tie with Everton: 'The game I was really disappointed with was the fifth round cup tie at Everton in February. There were nine fouls against him, with Mikel Arteta committing six of them on his own, and still no one got booked. It was absolutely ridiculous. It is an unfortunate issue we have to deal with, but the one thing it tells you is he gives defenders problems. If they have to foul him and bring him down all the time, it tells you he is doing well.'

Cristiano was slightly more concerned about the number of players who were copycatting his tricks: 'There is one thing that annoys me. I don't like people copying my tricks. I would never, for example, copy Ronaldinho if I saw him doing something on the pitch. I see football as an art and all the players are artists. If you are a top artist the last thing you would do is paint a picture that someone has already painted. I would never dream of looking at Ronaldinho and trying to emulate him. I would be offended if he tried to copy one of my tricks. Different tricks come naturally to gifted players and we must concentrate on developing our own natural talents rather than try and be someone else.'

He rooted this in his youth in Madeira: 'It's all down to street football. We'd eat, drink and breathe football. I always felt comfortable on the ball and have always had the belief that if you put one man or five men in front of me I could go past them all. I used to invent new tricks that I could try in my next game and I still do the same thing today.'

In fact, during Euro 2004 he explained his art form:

'I am at my happiest in life when I have the ball at my feet. I don't know how to explain it. It is as though the ball becomes a part of me. It is just a natural thing and something I find very difficult to control because much of my game is instinctive. I just don't think about it.

The coaches of Manchester United and Portugal have spoken to me about the way I play. They have been in the game a lot longer than me, they know what is required and so I listen to their words and try to learn. I know what they say is in the interests of the team, but I think that sometimes I have to be given the chance to express myself.'

May 21 Arsenal O–O Manchester United [aet Arsenal win 5–4 pens] FA Cup Final 2005

With no silverware for the Old Trafford faithfull, Fergie and United were determined to win the FA Cup against the enemy they had already trounced twice in the league. With Thierry Henry out and Wenger playing a labouring Dennis Bergkamp as a target man in a 4-5-1 formation, it looked like a shoo-in for United.

United decided not to kick Arsenal off the pitch but play them off it... which they did, with Ronaldo and Rooney rampant. Unfortunately for United, despite peppering Jens Lehmann's goal, they couldn't score. Lehmann played out of his skin and it was just one of those 'that's football' afternoons. United's keeper Roy Carroll didn't have to make one save in ordinary time. In fact, apart from turning a free kick from substitute Robin van Persie round the post, he didn't have much more to do in extra time either.

Penalties!!!!! Blast them, place them, dummy the keeper. Meanwhile, the keeper can on the assumption that at least one will be blasted straight at him hold his ground, he can try to read the taker or go early, guessing what way the taker will place it. Some keepers ensure that their guess is an informed one because they study the video tapes of all the penalties that they can find.

On this occasion, Lehmann guessed right on United's second, saving Paul Scholes' low drive into the left-hand corner of the net. Everyone's nerve held with Ronaldo and Rooney giving Lehmann no chance. Keane took United's fifth. Vieira followed him – he blasted it home. 5–4 Arsenal. For United, it was a crying shame and both Cristiano Rooney slummocked on the pitch with tears in their eyes. Who says professional footballers are only in it for the money! Not even Wenger took much pride in the result.

In close season, there was some speculation about Ronaldo moving to Real Madrid. His Portugal team-mate, Deco Maniche publicly asked him to come to Barca: 'He is a great player and it would be much better that he plays for us in Barcelona.' However, Cristiano re-affirmed his wish to stay with United, although he didn't actually sign till November.

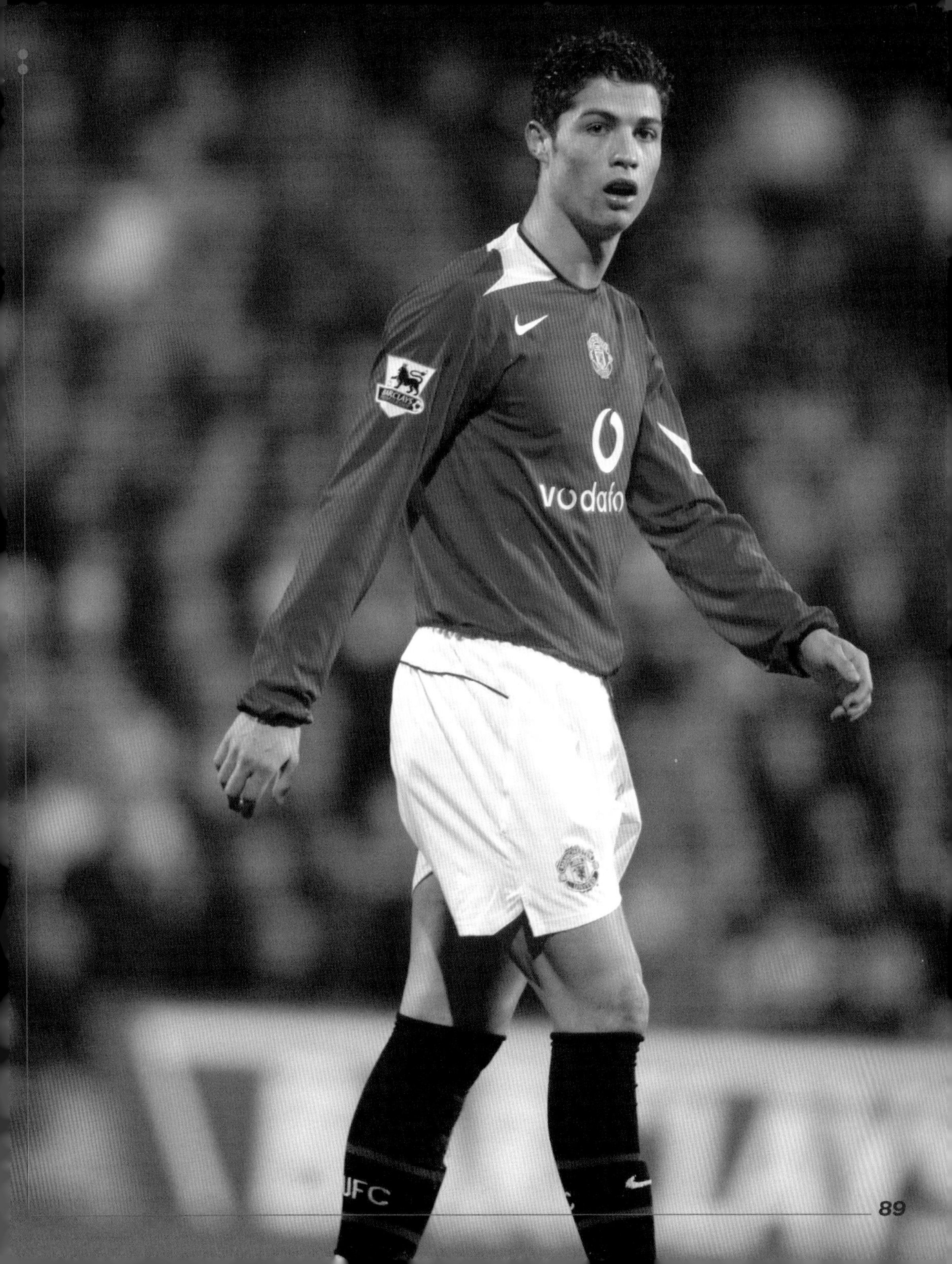

In the new season, Scolari picked him to play against Russia in a World Cup qualifying match and while he was in Moscow his father, Dinis, died on September 6th after a long illness. Cristiano played the match and went back to Madeira to attend the funeral. It proved to be a difficult time for him and looking back in March he said of that period:

'Obviously it has been really, really hard to take since my father died. Psychologically it was very tough. If you are not feeling well mentally because of something as awful as that, you will take that on to the pitch whether you like it or not and whether you are strong or not. It will affect you no matter what. I loved him the most in the world and it was a very difficult time for me. I had some poor matches because, psychologically, I wasn't right for matches. But life goes on and I am looking to the future. These things happen to everybody.

'Nobody has a heart of iron. That's life. To cope with it is one of the experiences in life that make you stronger.

In early September, at the awards ceremony of FIFPro (the worldwide representative organisation for professional players) both Ronaldo and Rooney received Young Player of the Year – Rooney voted by the players and Ronaldo by the general public. Ronaldinho was voted World Player of the Year.

Ronaldinho with Chelsea's John Terry

But there was to be little comfort for Cristiano in the coming months. United slumped badly partly because of injuries but suspensions and loss of form played their part. In the background were the controversial repercussions of US sports tycoon Malcolm Glazer finally gaining control of

Receiving the FIFPro World XI Player Award 2005

the club. Chelsea looked good in the Premiership and indifferent results in the Champions League suggested United would not get through the group stage. This proved to be the case. Against Benfica in late September they scraped through 2–1, although Cristiano played well. It was the return in December at Lisbon that put them out and proved the low spot in Cristiano's football career.

He relished the chance of playing against Sporting's rivals and also keeping United in the tournament. George Best had just died and it was against Benfica that Best had played such a dazzling part in winning the the European Cup in 1968. In trying too hard Ronaldo lost his way. He reverted to being a show pony but one whose tricks were all dressage. He was ridiculed by the home crowd and booed by the United contingent for losing possession.

Even on a yellow, he persistently argued with the referee. Not unwisely Ferguson hauled him off in the 67th minute. Benfica fans, already 2–1 up jeered him to the rooftop. He responded by giving them the finger and was reported to FIFA for his troubles. United did not even have the cushion of UEFA Cup to help offset the debts of the Glazier leverage: for the first time in 10 years Old Trafford did not host any European action in the second part of the season.

It was only two weeks since the Metropolitan Police Service had announced that after examining the evidence the Crown Prosecution Service had decided not to pursue charges against Ronaldo for serious sexual assault against two women in October. The incident

happened after the game with Fulham, a 5-goal thriller won by United in which Ronaldo only came on for the last 15 minutes. That evening he and his cousin had picked up two French escort girls, then took them back to his £1000-a-night suite at Soho's Sanderson Hotel where they had consensual sex . Ronaldo has his money's worth as he went with both of them. However, the next day they claimed they had been raped.

He said about his arrest as well he might: 'I've been stitched up. I had nothing to do with these women. I can't believe what's being alleged.'

And if that wasn't enough for the troubled manager, after attacking some of his team-mates in a spineless 4–1 defeat at Middlesbrough at the end of October Roy Keane left the club. He had been sidelined since mid-September with a broken metatarsal in his left foot but when he started to resume training he was also involved in a spat with assistant coach Carlos Queiroz. After 12 years of patrolling United's midfield, often like some psychotic Serbian warlord, Fergie decided enough was enough and Keane, who didn't need pushing, went immediately on September 18th.

In the Boro match, Ronaldo had come on as sub for South Korean Ji-Sung Park for the last 30 minutes, but Keane hadn't turned on him. His criticisms were aimed at the defence, in particular Rio Ferdinand and Darren Fletcher. No one criticised Ronaldo for being spineless, the two weaknesses in his game were showboating and not scoring enough.

He is aware of both. In March 2006 he said: 'My game has matured.

'I admit I did over-indulge on the tricks at times. I know the fans think I do it too much but I want them to know I am working on it. In the past I have got over-excited and got carried away.

'I sometimes did it at the wrong times. I know the crowd love it at the right times and I have tried to concentrate on that. If we are drawing or are in trouble then that is no time for me to be doing some fancy footwork.'

United's one bit of silverware for the 2005/06 season was the runt of the domestic tournaments, the League Cup: on February 26th, some eight days after Liverpool knocked them out of the FA Cup United steamrollered Wigan 4–0. It was all Rooney, who scored the first and last but Ronaldo took an emphatic 3rd. An error from Stephane Henchoz allowed Saha to find Cristiano in that familiar area where he had scored some crucial goals for Portugal. This time it was a low, fierce, skimming shot that he rifled into the corner. He wheeled away and took his shirt off to reveal even better definition in his upper body: he'd clearly been doing some bodybuilding in the gym.

He talks about how the Gaffer reckons he should be putting away 15-20 a season. The previous season he bagged 9 and this one 11. 'I have been working hard to get more goals into my game,' he said. 'I was looking forward to it happening and now it finally has. It didn't seem to happen for me before but now I am in my stride I want to keep it going. My goal is always to work and help the team first and foremost but I can do that by scoring as well.

'It is a unique feeling and I want more of it.'

United's late charge on Chelsea finished disappointingly and 'The Special One' handed his second Premiership title in two seasons on a platter to his Russian paymaster. It was finally sealed with a 3–0 drubbing of United at Stamford Bridge. However, the match will be remembered more for the innocuous tackle on Rooney by Portugal international Paulo Ferreira that left England's World Cup hope on the turf clutching his right foot in agony. Just 42 days before England open their World Cup bid and the curse of the metatarsal strikes again. On the same weekend, Phil Scolari rejected the FA's overtures for him to take over the England squad after Eriksson leaves. Portugal was making all the World Cup news.

Portugal are 20-1 and England 8-1 but they have Scolari not Eriksson as coach, and Big Phil will be out to prove a point. Cristiano Ronaldo is also coming into his own. Ronaldo could come on song in this world Cup: he has the dazzling skills and the warrior temperament that can turn a tournament. Who looks the better bet: Portugal with Scolari and Ronaldo or England with Eriksson and an injured Rooney?

United will be back in the European League next year with a committed Ronaldo: 'United have supported me all the way this season and for that I am grateful, he said. They have stood by me and been there for me and I want to repay them for that. They brought me to England and tried to make me a better player and they have worked hard and put the work in to do that with me. There is nobody else who could make me what I am now and I am really thankful.

'I will repay the faith.'